What is a
Patent

Fourth Edition

 AMERICANBARASSOCIATION

Intellectual Property
Law Section

Cover and interior design by ABA Design

Printed in the United States of America.

27 26 25 24 23   5 4 3 2 1

ISBN 978-1-63905-361-2
e-ISBN 978-1-63905-362-9

Discounts are available for books ordered in bulk. Special consideration is given to state bars, CLE programs, and other bar-related organizations. Inquire at Book Publishing, ABA Publishing, American Bar Association, 321 N. Clark Street, Chicago, Illinois 60654-7598.

www.shopABA.org

Contents

The Patent Grant and the Meaning of Patents

A patent is an official document granted by the federal government conveying to the recipient, called the patentee, specific rights named in the document and in the federal patent statutes. These rights are known as patent rights and are clearly defined in the statute (35 U.S.C. §154) as: "the right to exclude others from making, using, offering for sale, or selling the invention throughout the United States or importing the invention into the United States. . . ." The key term in the statute is the words "right to exclude," which is an essential feature of any property right. Thus, a patent is a grant of intellectual property rights by the United States government that permits the patent owner to stop others from exploiting the patented invention.

A patent includes three essential components: (1) drawings; (2) a written description or specification that describes and explains the patented invention; and, finally but most importantly; (3) claims, which define that which the patent right covers. In other words, the claims of a patent define the extent of the intellectual property right, which is granted by the United States government, and from the practice of which others can be excluded.

An essential feature of a patent is its limited life, as required by the U.S. Constitution. Congress sets a time limitation for each type of patent that may be obtained, at the end of which the patent right expires. In this way, the patent owner has a limited term for exercise of the right to prevent others from making, using, offering for sale, selling, or importing the patented invention. However, the public benefits as well because, after the patent expires, the public is free to practice the invention patented, the patentee no longer having the right to exclude anyone from making, using, or selling the invention of the patent. Equally important, because the inventor must describe the invention and how to practice it in the patent document, and because patents are published documents available to review by all when granted, the knowledge set forth in the patent becomes available to everyone.

Why are these documents called "patents"? The word "patent" means open, exposed, or evident. Our concepts of patents came from England and were included in our Constitution. In England, long before the American Revolution, it was an established practice and part of the law for the Crown to grant special privileges or monopolies by means of "Letters Patent," which were the documents open to public inspection setting forth such grants.

Such "Letters Patent" were granted for limited times for new inventions within the realm. With the passage of time, the phrase "Letters Patent" became shortened to the term "patent," but both mean the same thing.

Types of Patents

The U.S. Patent and Trademark Office (USPTO) issues three types of patents: utility patents, design patents, and plant patents.

Utility patents are the most widely known and are issued for new and useful inventions or discoveries relating to:

1. Processes;
2. Machines;
3. Manufactures;
4. Compositions of matter; or
5. Improvements in any of the above.

Utility patents are granted for a term beginning on the date the patent issues and ending 20 years from the date the application for the patent was filed in the United States or, if the patent claims priority from an earlier-filed U.S. application, 20 years from the date the earliest such U.S. application, other than a U.S. provisional patent application, was filed. (The term of a U.S. patent granted on an application filed prior to June 8, 1995, would end either 17 years from the date of issue or at the end of the 20-year term as described above, whichever is later, subject to any disclaimer of a terminal portion of the term of the patent prescribed by law (terminal disclaimer).)

Design patents are granted for any new, original, and ornamental design of an article of manufacture (that is, the way an article looks, not the way an article is used or works or functions). Since May 13, 2015, design patents in the United States are granted for a term of 15 years from the date of application for the design patent.

Plant patents are granted to whoever invents or discovers and asexually reproduces any distinct and new variety of plant (that is, distinct and new plants that are reproduced by means other than from seeds, such as by the rooting of cuttings, layering, budding, or grafting), including cultivated spores, mutants, hybrids, and newly found seedlings, other than a tuber propagated plant or a plant found in an uncultivated state. The term of a plant patent is the same as that of a utility patent—that is, 20 years from the filing date of the patent application.

Other Features of Patents

A patent is far more than simply a legal document. It is also a technical publication and a sales brochure. It is a technical document because it is required to contain a written description of the patented invention sufficient to permit anyone interested in the field to which the patent pertains to make and use (practice) the invention by reading the patent. Thus, issued patents provide a wealth of technical information for the public that is often unavailable elsewhere. A patent is also analogous to a sales brochure because it describes what was known before, commonly referred to as the "prior art," and then demonstrates how the invention of the patent improves or advances the known state of the art.

Traditionally, the original patent document was sent to its owner and was in the form of a set of printed pages and drawings (if any) that are bound together with a red ribbon fixed under a gold seal. As of April 18, 2023, the USPTO began publishing and issuing electronic patent grants (eGrants) to patent recipients; in other words, the official copy of patent grants is issued by the USPTO in an electronic format. Bound paper versions of the printed patent are still available from the USPTO, which is a part of the Commerce Department, for a nominal fee. Although the USPTO is part of the Commerce Department, which is located in Washington, D.C., since 2003 the official mailing address of the USPTO is Commissioner for Patents, P.O. Box 1450, Alexandria, VA 22313-1450, and its current physical location is in Crystal City, Virginia, just a few minutes from Reagan National Airport. Libraries in a number of major cities throughout the United States have collections of U.S. patents. U.S. patents that have issued since 1790 are available over the Internet from the USPTO website at www.uspto.gov.

The Value of Patents

One need only consider the cotton gin, the telegraph, the telephone, the airplane, the transistor, the computer, the cell phone, and a host of other inventions, all of which were patented, to realize that an essential cornerstone of the American success story is the framework for innovation provided by the patent system. For their disclosure of the invention in the patent document, the inventor is rewarded in the grant of the patent with the right to exclude others from practicing the invention claimed and, thus, is encouraged to come forth with new developments. The public benefits because, through the issuance of patents, knowledge of inventions and the technology disclosed is made available to everyone.

But the value of the patent itself can be no greater than the commercial value of the invention covered by the patent. It is the invention described and claimed in a patent and the market for the products or processes based on that invention that determine the value of the patent and not vice versa. Thus, the potential for monetary return to the patent owner lies in the commercial importance of the patented invention. An inventor will reap a monetary reward from a patent only if the invention ultimately meets with consumer acceptance.

The benefits to the public from the patent system can be enormous. Besides stimulating inventions, patents provide, through the right to exclude others from practicing the invention patented, the ability to attract the capital and effort required to develop inventions into perfected and marketable form. Patents for pioneer inventions often provide the foundation for entire new industries. Even patents covering minor improvements of a product or process may have significant value if the improvement results in a product or process either strongly preferred over competing products or one that is less expensive to manufacture or use.

How to Evaluate an Invention

Normally, evaluation of an invention is rather speculative. However, a few tests can be applied that may eliminate some ideas from further serious pursuit. These tests relate to the product that embodies or results from the invention.

Careful study should be given to the required investment for making a new product or, alternatively, to the necessary changes in existing production facilities. The advertising budget that will be required to change public buying habits to accept a new product is important. The potential size of the market should also be considered. Finally, a study should be made to predict the likely profit from the product. In sum, to determine the potential value of a patent, it is necessary to make a comprehensive business evaluation of the resulting product and its cost of production.

Although the value of a patent depends primarily on the commercial importance of the invention or discovery, there are other important considerations. The credibility associated with a discovery is a primary factor in attracting help to exploit it. A successful inventor acquires credibility in the same fashion as a successful painter or writer. In the absence of prior success, inventors must build credibility by proving their invention or discovery is worthy of exploitation. For example, a certain amount of credibility may result from the completion of an operating model. Usually, more credibility is gained with a production prototype. A favorable sales history for a patented product builds credibility. In other words, any step that concretely bridges the gap between a conceived idea and actual commercial exploitation tends to build credibility.

Timing is another element that affects the value of an invention. United States patents are enforceable for a limited period of time. At the end of that time, patent rights in the invention expire, and the invention usually can be freely practiced by anyone. A variety of economic, production, and management factors may come into play to shift the period of patent protection away from the period when an invention is commercially important. For example, the marketing period for a toy often is short-lived and may have passed even before a patent is granted. In those industries where change is expensive and time consuming, such as the automotive industry, actual production methods may lag current available technology by a period that is much longer than the life of a patent. Thus, the value of a patent can be greatly influenced by the patterns for change that exist for specific products and industries.

Unfortunately, many inventors often grossly underestimate the cost and difficulty of commercializing their inventions and overestimate market size and the chances of purchaser acceptance. Thus, an inventor must be prepared to face and overcome numerous difficulties before an invention returns a monetary reward. The inventor must be willing to work hard to realize any reward.

Before proceeding to obtain a patent, however, it is well to know what a patent is not and, further, what a patent cannot do.

What a Patent Is Not

A clearer understanding of just what a patent is requires consideration of what a patent is not. For example, a patent is not a trademark or copyright, these being three distinct fields of intellectual property law having little to do with one another, although there is some overlap with regard to the configuration or trade dress of a product. One who owns a trademark has the right to exclude others from using a confusingly similar trademark in commerce in such a manner as to confuse the public as to the source or origin of goods (or services) bearing the mark. Whether the goods are patented has nothing to do with rights afforded by trademark law.

A copyright permits the copyright owner to exclude others from copying the copyrighted material (such as books, plays, music, statues, motion pictures, television programs, computer programs), but copyright protection does not extend to an underlying invention or idea that might be described in the copyrighted matter. Thus, a copyright could be used to prevent others from copying a book describing an invention, but the copyright could not be used to prevent someone from using the knowledge set forth in the book and then making, using, or selling the invention. For example, a copyrighted book may fully describe a lawnmower, but no one could be stopped from building a lawnmower as taught by the book on the basis of copyright law.

It is also important to know that owning a patent on an invention does not confer a right to make, use, sell, offer to sell, or import the invention. What is granted is strictly the legal right to exclude others from doing so. For example, although a patent may be obtained on a new invention, the manufacture and sale of that invention can infringe a different patent owned by someone else. As another example, new drugs are patented all the time, but Food and Drug Administration approval is required before these patented drugs can be marketed. Furthermore, a patent is not self-enforcing. The government will not take any positive action on behalf of the patent owner. The government simply grants the right to exclude others from practicing the invention patented and leaves it to the patent owner to enforce the right—if it can be done. The government's role in case of a patent infringement suit is the provision of the federal judicial system, wherein such suits can be brought.

A patent is not necessarily worth anything. Given that a patent simply grants the right to exclude, its value rests entirely upon the utility of the invention and the desire of others to use it or to be in possession of the right to exclude. That is, someone might want to buy the patent from its owner. A patent is simply a document and not an invention. The invention is that which is described and claimed in the patent. It is also important to note that a patent may describe an additional invention or inventions beyond what is covered by the claims of the patent.

A patent cannot be kept secret or suppressed from public disclosure. An essential aspect of obtaining a patent is that a full and complete disclosure of the invention is made, so that others may practice it when the patent expires (absent some superior right in others). United States patent applications are normally published to the public 18 months after filing, unless no foreign counterpart applications will be filed and a request for nonpublication is filed with the U.S. patent application. Suppression of a patent, in the sense of secrecy, is simply a misconception. The most a patent owner can do in this regard is fail to commercialize the invention or refuse to allow others to do it by refusing to grant licenses. Inventions, of course, may be suppressed by keeping them out of use and secret, but patents can neither be kept secret nor suppressed.

The geographic extent of enforcement of a U.S. patent is limited to the 50 states and U.S. territories and possessions. Thus, a U.S. patent cannot be enforced in Canada, Japan, Europe, or any other foreign country However, the importation of products from abroad that infringe a U.S. patent may be stopped, and the infringer may be sued here. Also, the United States has ratified several treaties that provide significant advantages for those wishing to seek foreign patent protection based on a patent application filed in the United Sates. The details and provisions of such treaties are beyond the scope of this book but can be explained by a patent lawyer. As yet, there is no such thing as a true "international patent."

The grant of a patent does not provide any assurance that practice of the patented invention will not infringe a patent owned by another. For example, a patent might be granted for an improvement to a previously patented device, but practice of the improvement invention might infringe the claims of the earlier patent on the device. Similarly, when a patent expires, it is not always true that the invention may be freely exploited by anyone. There could very well be another unexpired patent having claims that would be infringed by one practicing the invention of the expired patent.

What Sort of Invention Is Patentable?

Once it is determined that there is a real, potential market for a product or process, and that good business judgment suggests that it should be commercialized, and that patent protection is desirable for the invention, the question to be asked is: Can the product or process be protected from imitators after it is revealed to the public? In other words, can the invention be patented?

Not every invention is patentable in the United States. To be patented, an invention must fall within the categories of patentable subject matter as discussed above.

In general, the USPTO is liberal in applying the limitations of these invention categories, provided that an invention is presented in a suitable fashion. For example, over the years patents have been granted on automobile parking structures, drive-in theaters, slot machines, and a host of computer-related applications.

Perhaps a better understanding of what kinds of developments may be patentable, if they meet the other requirements of the law, can be explained by indicating some of the things that are not patentable. Unpatentable subject matter includes business forms, perpetual motion machines, promotional advertising schemes, intended results of desired goals, functions (without apparatus), nebulous or abstract concepts or ideas, and laws of nature (as distinguished from applications of such laws). To summarize, desired functions are not patentable. It is the thing or the method that can be patented, not the result.

Regardless of the type of invention for which a patent is sought, there are three general requirements for patentability that are critically important. A patentable invention must be (1) useful, (2) new (novel), and (3) unobvious. The useful and new requirements have been well-established understood. The unobvious requirement is more amorphous. The section of the statute involved (35 U.S.C. §103) states it this way:

> A patent may not be obtained . . . if the differences between the subject matter sought to be patented and the prior art are such that the subject matter as a whole would have been obvious at the time the invention was made to a person having ordinary skill in the art to which said subject matter pertains.

To determine the "obviousness" of a discovery, one must first identify the prior art (earlier patents and publications). Locating the most pertinent prior art is not easy, what with all of the widespread public technological activity around the world. As a practical matter, one can never be positively certain of having located the most pertinent prior art in the abundance of technical knowledge and publications. However, any determination of patentability must be based upon some known prior art. With the known prior art in mind, patentability is determined by asking whether the invention would have been obvious to a hypothetical person of ordinary skill in the field who is aware of that prior art. To be patentable, an invention must differ from the prior art in a way that is not just an obvious change or addition. In considering the question, people may disagree on the abilities expected of the fictitious "person of ordinary skill," or on the content of the prior art, or on the conclusion that the hypothetical person of ordinary skill would reach. Any such disagreement is likely to result in a disagreement on the patentability of the invention in question. It remains an open question until decided by the court of last resort.

Who May Obtain a Patent?

Patents are granted only to certain individuals. Who are such persons? Only the first and original inventor (or those asserting rights obtained from the inventor) can properly obtain a U.S. patent. A person who merely recognizes the commercial merits of an existing product or who discovers it in a prior document or in a foreign country may not properly receive a patent; it must have been invented by that person. A corporation or business organization may not pursue patent protection on a development independently of the inventor. However, it is common practice for employed inventors to assign patent rights to their employers. Many employers make assignment a condition of employment, usually in their employment agreement.

The law recognizes that an invention may be made by one, two, or a greater number of persons. Accordingly, patent applications frequently name joint inventors. Problems may arise in this situation, but the problems can be solved. Specifically, unless there is an agreement or assignment of the patented invention to one of the inventors or to a third party, each inventor has the right to exploit the invention with no duty to account to the other inventor or inventors for their actions. This is true regardless of the percentage of the patent any one joint inventor may own. In addition, no one of the joint inventors has the right to exclude any of the other joint inventors from practicing the patented invention due to the right of the other joint inventor or inventors to use the invention and grant licenses to others. Thus, if possible, the rights and obligations of joint inventors should be defined by an agreement or the patent should be assigned to a single entity.

Occasionally, it happens that two or more independent inventors come up with the same invention at about the same time. Who gets the patent? Under the America Invents Act of 2011, after March 16, 2013, the inventor who first files their patent application receives priority to be awarded the patent. Before that law became effective, if two or more persons filed patent applications seeking patents for the same invention, only the first, true, and original inventor (or group of inventors) to "conceive" the invention and undertake steps diligently to reduce it to practice was entitled to the patent (sometimes after a USPTO proceeding called an "interference," to determine the first true inventor). The change in the U.S. law under the America Invents Act was made to bring the United States into harmony with most foreign patent systems.

Thus, an inventor in the United States should try to file their application with the USPTO as soon as they have determined that their invention is eligible for a patent. Although the U.S. patent law still allows inventors a one-year grace period to file a patent application after the first public disclosure of their invention (for example, in a publication or at a public conference), under the U.S. first-inventor-to-file system, if an inventor waits to file a patent application under the one-year grace period, and another inventor files an intervening patent application, then the first party filing the application will be entitled to receive the patent, not the inventor who may have been entitled to the patent under the first-to-invent system.

When May One Apply for a Patent?

Time is important, both as it relates to the activities of the inventor and the discoveries of others. Considering the possible history in the discovery of the wheel may help explain some of the time limits for patentability.

Initially, the first inventor of the wheel may have merely recognized the problems associated with moving large loads on rolling logs (the prior art). With only the recognition of the need for a better structure, a patent application would not yet be timely; a patentable invention had not yet been made. A patent application is not proper until a working form of an invention has been fully conceived. At a time when the complete invention is mentally pictured—that is, fully conceived in an operating form—the inventor may properly pursue patent protection.

Continuing with the example of the wheel, quite independently of an effort to obtain patent protection, the inventor might have published a description of the invention or may have built a wagon and gone into the moving business. Such activities would raise another question of timing. Under U.S. law, a patent application must be filed within one year after the invention first is described in any publication, placed on sale, sold, or used publicly. The general rule for this one-year grace period is based on the philosophy that the inventor abandons the patent rights if a proper patent application is not filed within one year from disclosure or commercial activity with respect to the invention or discovery. There are some exceptions to this rule, as in the case of legitimate experimental use to perfect or develop the invention.

As another timing consideration, any publication or public use of an invention that takes place before the filing of an application in the United States may block the inventor from obtaining a valid patent in some foreign countries, most of which apply an "absolute novelty" standard—that is, one does not, in most foreign countries, have a one-year grace period from the time of first disclosure in which to file an application, as is provided under U.S. law.

An inventor may keep the invention secret for some period of time and still obtain a patent. However, a long delay in applying for a patent may result in the loss of all patent rights if the invention is determined to have been suppressed.

Generally, it is wise to keep careful records of the invention and its development, which should be signed by a witness, and to file an application for a patent at the earliest practical time, preferably before any public description, commercial development, or public use of the invention.

How to Obtain a Patent

The steps involved in obtaining a patent include preparing a disclosure of the invention; conducting a patentability search on the invention (not mandatory but, generally, advisable); preparing and filing a formal nonprovisional patent application in the USPTO; prosecuting the application in the office; and, finally, issuing the patent.

If desired, a provisional patent application may be filed before a nonprovisional patent application is filed, but filing a provisional patent application starts a 12-month deadline in which the applicant must file a corresponding nonprovisional application for patent to benefit from the earlier filing of the provisional application. A provisional patent application helps protect a new invention from being copied during the 12-month period before a formal nonprovisional patent application is filed. It is intended to give an inventor time to pitch the idea, test its commercial feasibility, or refine a product before committing to the expensive and time-intensive process of a formal application. It allows an inventor to describe the invention as "patent pending." But failing to convert a provisional application to nonprovisional application before the 12-month deadline could result in the loss of protection for the invention.

An inventor may obtain a patent without the assistance of a patent lawyer or agent if the inventor so desires. However, ordinarily this is an unwise course of action. Patent law and procedure are complex, and valuable legal rights can easily be lost if the patent application and prosecution of that application are not handled carefully by one skilled in such matters.

Patent lawyers and patent agents (nonlawyers who are qualified to practice before the USPTO) can prepare and prosecute patent applications. Patent agents are not lawyers and cannot provide legal advice and assistance beyond preparing and prosecuting patent applications. To be registered, patent lawyers and agents must take and pass an examination given by the USPTO. A roster of patent lawyers and agents registered to practice before the USPTO, listing the individuals alphabetically, is available at a nominal cost from the Superintendent of Documents, U.S. Government Printing Office, Washington, D.C. 20402, and is also available from the UPTO Office of Enrollment and Discipline (https://www.uspto.gov/about-us/organizational-offices/office-general-counsel/office-enrollment-and-discipline-oed).

The major cost of obtaining a patent is the lawyer's charges. Ordinarily, this will be based upon the amount of lawyer time involved in preparing and prosecuting the application. Different patent lawyers may charge different fees, and some lawyers may consent to preparing a patent application for a flat fee after they sufficiently understand what the invention is and what the preparation of the application will entail. In any case, an inventor should not be hesitant about inquiring of the lawyer what their estimate might be as to the total fees in obtaining the patent if the patent is prosecuted through the USPTO in a fairly routine way. A patent lawyer can also advise the inventor of problems that could arise in the USPTO prosecution that could necessitate significantly greater costs, such as an appeal of a rejection from an examiner.

Prepare a Description of the Invention

Lawyers charge for their time, and patent lawyers are no exception. Therefore, an inventor can save a great deal of time and money by making the lawyer's job easier. A few hours spent by the inventor at the beginning may result in hundreds of dollars of savings and a better application in the end.

It is relatively easy for the typical inventor to organize their materials, and the inventor can help the patent lawyer by preparing a written description, drawings, and perhaps a model, if practical, of the invention. At a minimum, the disclosure to the patent lawyer should include a description of known relevant prior art inventions and pertinent information contained in issued patents and publications, along with a detailed description of the best mode of practicing the invention. If there are some likely alternative embodiments of the invention, those also should be described. The inventor does not have to detail each and every remotely possible embodiment, but describing alternatives or modifications helps the lawyer to draft claims adequate to provide good protection for the invention. The disclosure should be clear. It is not necessary that it be typewritten. A legible, carefully handwritten disclosure, including drawings, is usually adequate. A good disclosure is not necessarily long. If the inventor is unsure whether some detail should be included in the disclosure, it should be included. This will allow the patent lawyer to decide whether to make it part of the patent application. If the inventor has relevant prior art documents, copies of these should be provided to the lawyer, along with a description of their possible relevance to the new invention. Drawings prepared by the inventor should be clear and sufficiently detailed. It is good practice for the inventor to number the various parts of the invention and to key the number in with the written disclosure. If alternative embodiments of the invention are described in the disclosure, then drawings should be submitted illustrating them.

If a physical model or prototype of the invention exists, it should be provided to the patent lawyer. If this is not practical, photographs of the model may be used. Above all, an inventor should not conceal anything from their lawyer. Concealing facts may result in the issuance of an invalid or unenforceable patent.

Conduct a Patentability Search

Perhaps the most accessible and complete library of prior art is housed in the USPTO. The public is admitted to this library or "search room"; however, it is used primarily by professionals. Patent lawyers not in the Washington, D.C. area invariably have Washington, D.C. associates who can make various types of patent searches and who can obtain other types of information from the USPTO. United States patents that have issued since 1790 can be searched on the USPTO website (www.uspto.gov) and on other third-party websites. Although inventors may make their own preliminary search, it usually is wise to have an experienced professional perform the search.

In general, the cost of a patent search depends on the time it requires. In some instances, it may be practical to forego a search before filing a patent application. For example, if the subject matter is difficult to search, or the product has been scheduled for production, or the inventor has a keen knowledge of the prior art, it may be prudent to forego a preliminary search.

If a search reveals that the invention is not patentable, then the cost of filing an application will be saved. If the search reveals that the invention may be patentable, the references located in the search can be used to provide useful background information and indicate the possible scope of potential patent claims.

Prepare and File the Patent Application

A patent application is the document filed with the USPTO for the purpose of obtaining a patent. Given that there are significant limitations on making changes in the application after it is filed—a strict rule against adding "new matter" to the application—it should be prepared with care. Both the inventor and attorney have legal obligations to ensure that the various parts of the application are correct and, to the best of their knowledge, are not misleading.

It is not necessary to construct a working model before filing a patent application. However, the effective preparation of a patent application is a demanding project, requiring full knowledge of a completely conceived invention. The patent application must disclose the best mode contemplated by the inventor for practicing the invention. Also, there is a duty to disclose all knowledge of pertinent "prior art," that is, references describing items already in the public domain (prior patents or published patent applications; other nonpatent literature such as articles, electronic publications, and on-line publications; other evidence of prior public uses or sales or offers to sell an item; or other evidence making an item otherwise available to the public). Also, as part of the application, the inventor must sign an oath or declaration stating recognition of a duty to disclose all material information to the USPTO. The patent application provides the foundation for defining the proper scope of patent protection that is to be granted.

The main parts of a nonprovisional patent application are a discussion of the background and prior art, a detailed description of the invention, drawings (if necessary) to aid in understanding the description, and the claims. Provisional patent applications need not include claims. In the background and prior art discussion, problems or shortcomings that have been experienced in practices or products known in the prior art should be described.

Many patent applications include drawings as part of the invention description, usually to illustrate the best embodiment of the invention. Patent applications on chemical compositions are one exception to that practice (although many chemical patent applications still include drawings). The drawings of a patent application must conform to established standards and are made by professional draftsmen. The style and technique for the drawings are different from the formats used in industry. As a consequence, patent drawings are made by specialists who work under the direction of the lawyer and are familiar with USPTO drawing requirements.

The written description of the invention must include adequate technical information, with the drawings, to permit one having ordinary skill in the art to practice the invention. Details about every part of the invention may not be required, so long as such details are well known or consist of standard, commercially available parts. The written description should include alternatives and equivalent structures that will also work in the invention.

Although claims are placed last in the patent application, their importance is first, because perfection in the rest of the application will be of little value if the claims do not properly cover the invention. This is not to say that there may not be remedies for imperfect claims under the right circumstances, but it is important that properly written claims of appropriate scope be present in the application. Most of the prosecution is devoted to having the claims written in acceptable form.

Usually, the most effective patent application results from a joint effort between the inventor and their patent lawyer. Of course, there are exceptions, and it is possible for a person to act on their own behalf, without a lawyer. When an application is prepared by a lawyer working with the inventor, there should be total communication. Specifically, it is important that the lawyer be given all the relevant information for the job. The preparation of a patent application can be compared to making a cake. Considerable assistance can be given to a cook by pre-measuring the ingredients, laying out the tools, and preparing the oven; but usually it is best for the cook to mix the ingredients. Somewhat similarly, in the preparation of a patent application, the inventor should provide the information but allow the lawyer to compose and draft the complex document. Drawings, photographs, written material, and oral discussions all may be helpful to educate the lawyer, depending on individual circumstances. Patent applications on complex subject matter normally should include at least one meeting between inventor and lawyer.

After a draft of the application is prepared, the lawyer should ask the inventor to review it carefully to determine whether there are corrections or changes to be made before it is placed in its final form for execution and filing in the USPTO. The formal papers (petition, oath or declaration, power of attorney) are prepared for the inventor's signature or execution. The complete application signed by the inventor is then sent or delivered to the USPTO along with the appropriate filing fee. Once the application is on file, the invention, if marketed, may be marked with the notice "patent pending," although the right to prohibit use of the invention by others does not mature until the patent is granted.

Provisional and Nonprovisional Patent Applications

An application for a U.S. patent may be either a provisional patent application or a nonprovisional patent application.

A provisional patent application may be filed without any formal patent claims, without an oath or declaration, and without any disclosure of known material prior art, all of which are required in a nonprovisional patent application. A provisional application must include, among other things, a cover sheet identifying the application as a provisional application, the names of all of the inventors, a written description of the invention, any drawings that are necessary to understand the invention, and a filing fee. A provisional application will not be examined for patentability and will not issue as a U.S. patent. The filing of a provisional application provides an early priority date for subsequently filed U.S. nonprovisional applications and foreign applications. The priority period provided by a provisional application is excluded from the calculation of the term of a U.S. patent that relies on the provisional application for priority. A provisional application cannot claim priority from a previously filed U.S. or foreign patent application and cannot be filed for design inventions. A "Patent Pending" notice may be used in connection with inventions that are the subject of a provisional patent application. A provisional application will automatically become abandoned 12 months after the filing date of the provisional application.

A provisional patent application is not to be confused with the mere filing of documents in the USPTO under the Disclosure Document Program. That was a service provided by the USPTO that allowed inventors to file a description of their invention with the USPTO to establish a date of invention under the now-superseded (since 2013) "first to invent" rule. The USPTO Disclosure Document Program has now ended.

If a provisional application has been filed, a nonprovisional application must be filed within 12 months of the filing date of the provisional application in order to claim priority from the provisional application filing date. A nonprovisional application can claim priority from more than one provisional application. A nonprovisional application must be filed with, among other things, at least one formal patent claim and an oath or declaration signed by the inventor(s). A nonprovisional application will be examined for issuance as a U.S. patent.

A nonprovisional application can be filed as the first application for the invention. There is no requirement that a provisional application must be filed before a nonprovisional application can be filed. However, as a provisional application need not include formal patent claims or an oath or declaration signed by the inventor(s), a provisional application often is filed when a patent application must be filed relatively quickly, such as if the invention is soon to be publicly disclosed and foreign filing rights are desired to be preserved or if the one-year grace period for a U.S. patent application is about to expire.

Prosecution of the Nonprovisional Patent Application

Patent applications filed in the USPTO are given serial numbers in chronological sequence. The filing date is also part of the identification for an application.

Within the USPTO, nonprovisional patent applications are assigned to examiners with specialized technical expertise. The examination of nonprovisional applications normally occurs in the order in which they are received by the examiner. Every effort is made by the USPTO to attain uniform and fair treatment of patent applications, and communications with the USPTO must meet certain standards and formalities.

In a typical case, the patent examiner first reviews the patent application for compliance with formal requirements. The next step is to consider the invention as claimed. With an understanding of the claimed invention, a search is made of earlier patents and publications (the prior art) to determine whether the claims of the patent application define subject matter that is patentable over the prior art. Traditionally, examiners are conservative, if not skeptical, in recognizing patentable subject matter. After determining an initial position, the examiner prepares a report, or Examiner's Action (commonly called an "Office Action"), explaining that position in a communication to the patent applicant. Usually, few, if any, claims are allowed in the first Office Action.

If the applicant has a patent lawyer, the Office Action is sent directly, and only, to the lawyer. The lawyer will then typically advise the inventor of the Office Action and request the inventor's assistance and instructions for responding to the examiner's position. For example, the inventor may be asked to review the prior art cited by the examiner and explain their response on the comparison of the prior art to the claimed invention. The applicant is given a time period for responding to the Office Action. The response might take the form of an argument seeking to change the examiner's position, with or without an amendment modifying the claims of the patent application.

After receiving the response to the Office Action, the examiner again considers the case and reviews the prior position on patentability. Although the matter may not be concluded at that stage, there usually are no more than two actions and responses before the question of patentability of the claims is resolved. Of course, the examiner may determine that the application simply is not directed to a patentable invention. Alternatively, the examiner may recognize the existence of a patentable invention and agree with the form and scope of the claims. A greater possibility is that the examiner concedes the invention to be patentable but disagrees with the lawyer on the scope of the claims that should be granted. Failing an agreement on any aspect, an appeal can be pursued. Frequently, however, agreement is reached, whereupon the patent application is ready to mature into, or "issue," as a patent. A "Notice of Allowance" results.

Issuance of the Patent

After the Notice of Allowance is issued, a "final fee" must be paid. A patent number and issue date will be assigned to an application and an Issue Notification will be mailed after the issue fee has been paid and processed by the USPTO. Under prior USPTO procedures, patents were normally issued within about four weeks after the issue fee was received. Under the new electronic issuance procedures beginning in 2023, this time may be reduced to as little as one week. From filing to issue, the average time a patent application is pending is usually more than 18 months, although this time varies depending on the technology concerned with the invention. Also, under the America Invents Act of 2011, the USPTO established procedures under which the examination of a patent application may be accelerated. An applicant may file a petition to make special under the accelerated examination program, which may reduce the pendency to as little as 12 months.

By long tradition, patents always are issued on a Tuesday. Also on Tuesday of each week, the USPTO publishes the *Official Gazette* abstracting all of the patents issued on that day. Patents are issued in numerical order.

Before the electronic issuance program began on April 18, 2023, the original paper copy of the patent would be mailed to the patent lawyer or patent agent, if either is used for the application process, or directly to the patentee, if there is no patent lawyer or patent agent involved. Under the electronic issuance program, patent grants are no longer issued on paper, so they are no longer mailed to the patent lawyer or patent agent or patentee at their correspondence address of record (although the USPTO did provide a paper copy of the electronic patent grant as a courtesy ceremonial copy, delivered to the patentee's correspondence address of record, during a transition period). Patent grant copies, including the ceremonial copy, are available for purchase from the USPTO at a nominal charge. The original ceremonial patent is an important document that should be kept with other, similarly important and valuable papers.

The issuance of a U.S. patent puts the inventor in the company of Thomas Edison (the incandescent electric lamp, among many others), the Wright brothers (the airplane), Stephanie Kwolek (Kevlar fiber), and other inventors who have held U.S. patents for their inventions and is an occasion that rightfully brings respect and admiration to the inventor. At the same time, the public benefits by having the inventor's disclosure of the new and useful discovery.

Maintenance Fees

Once a utility patent has issued, periodic maintenance fees must be paid to the USPTO in order to maintain the patent in force. Maintenance fees are due at each of the $3\frac{1}{2}$-, $7\frac{1}{2}$-, and $11\frac{1}{2}$-year anniversary dates from the date of issue of the patent. A six-month grace period is provided for the late payment of a maintenance fee upon the payment of an additional late fee. Maintenance fees are not required to be paid to maintain design patents and plant patents in force.

Exploitation of Patents

The need for creativity does not end with the issuance of a patent. Whether the inventor seeks to either license their invention or directly market the resulting product, success usually requires an innovative and intense effort. The process is likely to be difficult, and chances for success are statistically poor. This is true for the established innovator as well as the unknown independent inventor. The mere availability of a new product, even an exciting one, may not stimulate much interest from serious investors or purchasers. Develop credibility, use imagination, and make the effort. Thousands have been successful but rarely without initial setbacks and disappointments.

Because of the difficulties in marketing new inventions, independent inventors have sometimes turned to promoters for help. These promoters have variously identified themselves, for example, as invention developers, idea brokers, and technology or marketing consultants. Unfortunately, some invention promoters offering services to independent inventors have preyed on the unwary, making promises that they are incapable of keeping and then charging exorbitant fees. Financial loss and heartbreak have taught many inventors the lesson of caution in dealing with unscrupulous promoters.

Patent licensing offers a variety of possibilities. A license can be limited to a single company (exclusive) or nonexclusive licenses can be granted to several companies. Other aspects of licensing include the responsibility for enforcement, conditions of termination, foreign rights, related trade secrets, know-how, and the very important royalty payment. Licenses are common that provide for:

1. A single lump-sum royalty payment;
2. A royalty of a specified amount for each product produced under the license; or
3. A royalty in the form of a percentage of the receipts from the sale of the licensed subject matter.

Although royalty percentage rates are the most common form of license payments, the rates vary widely from fractional percentages to double-digit percentage figures, depending on the nature of the industry, production costs, the significance of the invention, and so on.

There are prohibitions on licensing, the violation of which can amount to patent misuse or antitrust violations. For example, a licensor should not fix prices, require the purchase of unpatented products for use with the patented item, regulate post-sale use of the patented product, or require royalty payments beyond the life of the patent. The law in this area is complex; this summary is merely to indicate the possibility of danger. Similarly, a patent holder should be aware that the details of a license could have profound consequences on the tax aspects of royalty payments.

Patents may also be sold to a willing buyer for a lump sum, on an ongoing royalty, or both.

Enforcement of Patents

Many conflicts involving patents are settled by negotiation. Failing the settlement of a conflict, a lawsuit for patent infringement may be brought in an appropriate federal district court. The objectives usually are damages (as from loss of sales or royalties) and an injunction against further infringement.

It is also possible for an alleged infringer to initiate legal action to attack the patent. This usually happens after a charge of infringement has been made by the patent owner against the alleged infringer. Usually in patent litigation, the rights granted to the patentee are reviewed and the infringement of such rights is determined.

In addition to attacking the validity of a patent in a federal district court, an accused infringer may challenge the validity of a patent by petition in the Patent Trial and Appeal Board (PTAB). The PTAB is a tribunal within the USPTO that decides patentability questions for issued patents in proceedings called AIA (America Invents Act) trials. AIA proceedings are complex matters and include three different types of review: *inter partes* review (IPR, by far the most common proceeding in the PTAB), post grant review, and covered business method review. After a petition for one of these reviews is submitted to the PTAB, the patent owner may respond to the petition, then the PTAB will determine whether to institute an AIA trial. If a trial is instituted, the petitioner and the patent owner will have opportunities to gather evidence and present additional briefing and request an oral hearing before the PTAB. At the conclusion of the trial, the PTAB will issue a final written decision, determining whether the challenged claims are unpatentable, usually within one year of the date the trial proceeding was instituted. Because the PTAB procedure is usually faster than a federal district patent infringement case, federal district judges may be asked to use their discretion to stay, or halt, an infringement case to allow the PTAB challenge to proceed.

The ultimate infringement suit is a very involved and expensive proceeding that may take several years. Pretrial discovery procedures in federal district court are liberal in allowing the parties to obtain very detailed information from each other. Perhaps as a result, high percentages of such cases are settled, and recent experience with alternative dispute resolution procedures has led to an increase in their use.

Alternatives to Patent Protection

Some inventions can be commercially exploited while being kept secret. For example, a product may not reveal a chemical process that is used to make the product. Also, in some instances, agreements for secrecy have been used successfully, as in the protection of computer software source code or algorithms. However, outside these possibilities, trade secrets (like all secrets) are difficult to keep. In general, one who learns a trade secret without wrongdoing (as by independent reverse engineering, discovery, or analysis) is legally free to use the knowledge.

Trademark and copyright protection do not cover inventions, as was explained earlier. Thus, a patent provides its owner with a unique package of rights that cannot be duplicated by any other legal document. Only a patent can stop others—whether they have copied the invention or have done their work independently—from making, using, offering for sale, selling, or importing the patented invention.

About the Author

Philip Swain is a patent attorney with more than 35 years' experience litigating patent cases in United States trial and appellate courts, including the International Trade Commission. He was a partner at two major law firms, based in Boston and Chicago, and now has his own law practice focused on alternative dispute resolution of intellectual property disputes. He is also an adjunct professor of law at Suffolk University Law School, where he teaches patent litigation.

Phil received his law degree from Northwestern University in Chicago in 1984, and his undergraduate degree in mechanical engineering from Tufts University in Medford, Massachusetts in 1981. After graduating from law school, he served as law clerk to the Honorable Giles S. Rich, Circuit Judge of the United States Court of Appeals for the Circuit. Phil has served on the ABA Section of Intellectual Property Law Council and chair of its Amicus and Patent Litigation Committees and Patent Division. He is a member of the Section's Books Editorial Board and Content Advisory Board. He has also served as President of the Federal Circuit Bar Association and Chair of the AIPPI-US Division of the American Intellectual Property Law Association (the international association for the protection of intellectual property),

About the ABA Section of Intellectual Property Law

From its strength within the American Bar Association, the ABA Section of Intellectual Property Law (ABA-IPL) advances the development and improvement of intellectual property laws and their fair and just administration. The Section furthers the goals of its members by sharing knowledge and balanced insight on the full spectrum of intellectual property law and practice, including patents, trademarks, copyright, design, and trade secrets. Providing a forum for rich perspectives and reasoned commentary, ABA-IPL serves as the ABA voice of intellectual property law within the profession, before policy makers, and with the public.

ABA Section of Intellectual Property Law (ABA-IPL)
Order today! Call 800-285-2221
Monday-Friday, 8:00 a.m. – 5:00 p.m., CT
or visit www.ambar.org/iplbooks.

Qty	Title	Regular Price	ABA-IPL Member Price	Total
____	ADR Advocacy, Strategies, and Practices for Intellectual Property and Technology Cases, 2nd Ed. (5370231)	$149.95	$119.95	$_____
____	ANDA Litigation, 3rd Ed. (5370243)	$379.00	$295.95	$_____
____	Antitrust Issues in Intellectual Property Law (5370222)	$149.95	$119.95	$_____
____	Arbitrating Patent Disputes (5370229)	$89.95	$74.95	$_____
____	Careers in IP Law (5370204) (The ebook is complimentary with ABA-IPL Section membership)	$24.95	$16.95	$_____
____	Commercialization of IP Rights in China (5370241)	$119.95	$95.95	$_____
____	A Comprehensive Patent Practice Form Book (5370260))	$139.95	$109.95	$_____
____	Computer Games and Immersive Entertainment, 2nd Ed. (5370239)	$89.95	$69.95	$_____
____	Copyright Litigation Strategies (5370228)	$369.00	$285.00	$_____
____	Copyright Remedies (5370208)	$89.95	$74.95	$_____
____	Copyright Termination Law (5370226)	$139.95	$109.95	$_____
____	Crash Course on U.S. Patent Law (5370221)	$39.95	$34.95	$_____
____	The DMCA Handbook, 2nd Ed. (5370234)	$79.95	$64.95	$_____
____	The Essential Case Law Guide to PTAB Trials (5370233)	$249.95	$199.95	$_____
____	The Essentials of Japanese Patent Prosecution (5370245)	$149.95	$119.95	$_____
____	Intellectural Property and Technology Due Diligence (5370236)	$219.95	$179.95	$_____
____	The Intellectual Property Law Handbook, 2nd Ed. (5620154)	$139.95	$109.95	$_____
____	IP Attorney's Handbook for Insurance Coverage in Intellectual Property Disputes, 2nd Ed. (5370210)	$139.95	$129.95	$_____
____	IP Protection in China (5370217)	$139.95	$109.95	$_____
____	IP Strategies for Medical Device Technologies (5370238)	$149.95	$119.95	$_____
____	IP Valuation for the Future (5370237)	$89.95	$59.95	$_____
____	The Law of Trade Secret Litigation Under the Uniform Trade Secrets Act, 2nd Ed. (5370242)	$369.95	$295.95	$_____
____	A Lawyer's Guide to Section 337 Investigations before the U.S. International Trade Commission, 4th Ed. (5370240)	$139.95	$109.95	$_____
____	Legal Guide to Video Game Development, 2nd Ed. (5370227)	$74.95	$59.95	$_____
____	A Legal Strategist's Guide to Trademark Trial and Appeal Board Practice, 4th Ed. (5370247)	$179.95	$144.95	$_____
____	New Practitioner's Guide to Intellectual Property (5370198)	$89.95	$69.95	$_____
____	Patent Claim Drafting Practice (5370259)	$179.95	$144.95	$_____
____	Patent Freedom to Operate Searches, Opinions, Techniques, and Studies (5370230)	$139.95	$109.95	$_____
____	Patent Neutral (5370232)	$89.95	$69.95	$_____
____	Patent Trial Advocacy Casebook, 3rd Ed. (5370124)	$149.95	$119.95	$_____
____	Patently Persuasive (5370206)	$129.95	$99.95	$_____
____	The Practitioner's Guide to the PCT, 2nd Ed. (5370261)	$139.95	$109.95	$_____

ABA Section of Intellectual Property Law (ABA-IPL)
Order today! Call 800-285-2221
Monday-Friday, 8:00 a.m. – 5:00 p.m., CT
or visit www.ambar.org/iplbooks.

Qty	Title	Regular Price	ABA-IPL Member Price	Total
_____	The Practitioner's Guide to Trials Before the Patent Trial and Appeal Board, 3rd Ed. (5370258)	$169.95	$139.95	$_____
_____	Pre-ANDA Litigation, 3rd Ed. (5370256)	$349.00	$259.00	$_____
_____	Preliminary Relief in Patent Infringement Disputes (5370194)	$119.95	$94.95	$_____
_____	Right of Publicity (5370215)	$89.95	$74.95	$_____
_____	Settlement of Patent Litigation and Disputes (5370192)	$179.95	$144.95	$_____
_____	Starting an IP Law Practice (5370202)	$54.95	$34.95	$_____
_____	Summary of Covenants Not to Compete (5370244)	$179.95	$144.95	$_____
_____	The Tech Contracts Handbook, 3rd Ed. (5370248)	$42.95	$33.95	$_____
_____	The Technology Transfer Law Handbook (5370211)	$220.00	$176.00	$_____
_____	Trademark and Deceptive Advertising Surveys, 2nd Ed. (5370255)	$189.95	$151.95	$_____
_____	What Is a Copyright (5370257)	$19.95	$16.95	$_____
_____	What Is a Patent (5370262))	$19.95	$16.95	$_____
_____	What Is a Trademark (5370250)	$19.95	$16.95	$_____

* Tax		$_____
** Shipping/Handling		$_____
TOTAL		$_____

Payment
❑ Check payable to the ABA
❑ VISA   ❑ Mastercard   ❑ American Express   ❑ Discover

Credit Card #_____ Exp._____

Signature_____

Name_____

Firm/Organization_____

Address_____

City_____ State_____ Zip Code_____

Phone_____ E-mail_____
(in case of questions about your order)

Please allow 5 to 7 business days for UPS delivery. Need it sooner? Ask about overnight delivery. Call the ABA Service Center at 800-285-2221 for more information.

Guarantee: If—for any reason—you are not satisfied with your purchase, you may return it within 30 days of receipt for a complete refund of the price of the book(s). No questions asked.

Please mail your order to:
ABA Publication Orders, 321 N. Clark St., 16th Floor, Chicago, Illinois 60654
Phone: 800-285-2221 or 312-988-5522 • Fax: 312-988-5568
E-mail: orders@abanet.org

Thank you for your order!

AMERICAN**BAR**ASSOCIATION
Intellectual Property
Law Section